Why I Don't Take Xanax

Why I Don't Take Xanax

Poems by

Christine Potter

© 2026 Christine Potter. All rights reserved.
This material may not be reproduced in any form, published,
reprinted, recorded, performed, broadcast,
rewritten or redistributed without
the explicit permission of Christine Potter.
All such actions are strictly prohibited by law.

Cover design by Shay Culligan
Cover image by Luca Bravo A. on Unsplash

ISBN: 979-8-90146-700-8
Library of Congress Control Number: 2026931469

Trademark Notice ~ Xanax® is a registered trademark of Viatris (or its subsidiaries/affiliates). The use of the trademarked name Xanax® in the title and throughout this book is for identification and descriptive purposes only. This book is not sponsored, endorsed by, or affiliated with Viatris or any of its subsidiaries. The author and publisher have no financial interest in the product or the company.

Kelsay Books
502 South 1040 East, A-119
American Fork, Utah 84003
Kelsaybooks.com

For my husband Ken, whose love, steadiness, and patience gave me a safe place to write and polish the poems in this book.

Acknowledgments

Thank you to the following publications, in which versions of these poems previously appeared:

After Happy Hour Poetry Prize, 2024: "Nana and the Squirrels"
Autumn Sky Poetry Daily: "Owls," "Trying to Read *The Gulag Archipelago* on My First Hundred-Degree Day," "Some Facts You Should Know About the Love of Music," "On the Seven Canonical Hours," "Why I Don't Take Xanax," "Sparrows, Starlings" (IBPC winner, May 2021)
Eclectica: "Fireworks," "Teaching a Writing Workshop at the School Where I Worked for Many Years"
Halfway Down the Stairs: "Forsythia"
Kestrel: "And So I Inhaled," "I'll Tell You a Secret"
The McNeese Review: "On 'Falling'"
Mobius, A Journal of Social Change: "What We Really Lost," "Another Poem About the Fourth of July"
The Rappahanock Review: "As If We Were Anything But"
Rattle: "Preacher's Traveling Organ"
Rattle Poets Respond: "I Want to Love the World," "On the Election," "Close Call," "My Sister's Birthday Is the Day After 9/11"
A River Sings: "And then, after you got the vaccine," "On the National Day of Mourning for the Covid Dead"
The Rockland County Business Journal: "As If We Were Anything But"
The Scarborough Presbyterian Newsletter: "Why I Don't Take Xanax"
Snakeskin: "At Brunch, My Mother Tells Me to Write About Mountains"
Third Wednesday: "My Late Mother Drinking Apple Martinis with J.S. Bach"

Contents

Owls	13
As If We Were Anything But	14
How Mom Dressed Us Up	16
TV, 1960	17
Vanishing Points	18
What I Want	19
On "Falling"	20
Making a 16mm Movie at the Cloisters	22
Fireworks	23
Forsythia, 1973	25
What He Was Bad at He Did Anyway	26
Trying to Read *The Gulag Archipelago* on My First Hundred-Degree Day	28
Junk Cedar	29
Home Renovation Show	30
Coming Back to Lead a Writing Workshop at the School Where I Once Worked	32
At Brunch, My Mother Tells Me to Write About Mountains	34
My Mother	36
Jimmy Carter Released from the Hospital After Fracturing His Pelvis	38
On the Glide Path	40
Driving North with My Husband	42
Dinner Time	43
I Was Sad This Morning and Now I Am Not	45
After	46
My Sister's Birthday Is the Day After 9/11	48
My Late Mother Drinking Apple Martinis with J.S. Bach	50

On the Seven Canonical Hours	52
Some Facts You Should Know About the Love of Music	54
Preacher's Traveling Organ	56
Singing Solo	57
Magdalene	58
My Cat Talks in Her Sleep	59
The Noisy Person I Am	60
Snapshots with Strangers	62
What We Really Lost	64
And then, after you got the vaccine	65
On the National Day of Mourning for the Covid Dead	66
Awakening Around Three, Lovestruck	68
Blessed Are Those Who Mourn	69
Blessed Are the Merciful	70
How Hate Spreads	72
Sparrows, Starlings	74
On the Election	76
Another Poem About the Fourth of July	77
I Want to Love the World	79
I Can't Lie to You	80
Close Call	82
I'll Tell You a Secret	84
Just Before Thanksgiving	85
All of Us New to Caution	86
The Feast of Busby Berkeley	88
Mostly, I'm Thinking of Ghosts	90
All Our Houses Are the Same House	92
Nana and the Squirrels	94
Why I Don't Take Xanax	97

Owls

I was talking to the owls again tonight.
It was like scrolling on social media—
hoo-HOO, hoo-HOO—and they liked it.

It was warmer today. The air felt like
a friend, and the creek sounded serious
and steady. I'd been inside until dusk.

I spoke with the owls, which my father
said flew off with unruly children—one
specific owl, actually: *The* Owl. We both

knew that wasn't true. His mother (tiny,
superstitious, Irish) used it to scare him.
Except he knew I'd be too smart to fool.

I was. I'm still angry at my father, but
not about that. Sometimes winter lets up
just a little and I miss him: hoo-HOO,

hoo-HOO. I talk to the owls. They answer
me back, outside with night just pulling
itself together, a few stars poking through.

As If We Were Anything But

Nobody gave me permission to write these words.
They are the opposite of the family credo: *nothing
we say in this house gets told to anyone outside it.*
As if we were anything but a bunch of intellectuals

losing their tempers. As if you didn't have to have
sex to have children. As if no one's secrets were
deeper than the silken, flesh-colored ottoman in
my mother's bedroom, with its top that opened,

revealing a dozen pairs of impractical shoes
unworn since before she was married. As if no one
else's grandmother had to inject her own thigh
with medicine to stop migraines. As if no one else's

father cheated—but I knew more about Nana's
needles than that; I'd seen how she pinched her
own fullness before she used one. As if no one's
mother chose not to get divorced, sharpened her

stenography skills and went back to work. As
if no one else's father taught her to develop film
in the darkroom anyway. As if I never turned into
your father's daughter after he did. As if any

of us knew how to do anything else, including me,
including now. As if I had never gazed into the
ghosts of my friends' faces in a sneaker-smelling
tray of processing fluid, under the orange safe light.

How Mom Dressed Us Up

Here's that picture again, flashgun splash in the
murk of our living room, my little sister a pink
and yellow Disney bunny, whiskers sketched on

her cheeks, mild, uncomplicated grin—but God
help the misplaced genie in her black and purple
sequined satin, arched, penciled eyebrows, mouth

painted scarlet as something spilled: me. Both of
us under ten. My sister stands, chin-high-happy,
a peck on the cheek about to happen, and I'm all

vamped-out on our old cabbage-rose couch, book
tight closed under one hand. My sulky lips barely
parted. I remember the stage makeup Mom took

out on Halloween, its odd smell not exactly sweet,
holding stiff-spine-still so she could turn me into . . .
what? Susan was an angel one year. World-weary

at eight, I'd forgotten which lamp to leap out of. Or
did Mom think I'd grant you a wish, two or three? I
knew *that* was pure nonsense. But hey, what'll it be?

TV, 1960

I didn't really like it but couldn't wait to get
home and watch anyway. TV was the kind of
division that came out evenly, afternoons
sorted into stories that resolved themselves

in thirty minutes, the rhythmic sound as I
twisted the knob to change channels: *voices,
static. Voices, voices, static.* Someone reading
the grey-suited headlines. A *Lucy* rerun I'd seen

already, the big *WAH* at the end, no rhumba
with the band for her. That was supposed
to be funny. Why was it funny when someone
cried? When I did, my dad said *boo-wah* and

giggled, sure as a laugh track. *We interrupt
this program for a bulletin from CBS news.*
I was home from school sick, reading and
listening at the same time, my mother's

gilt-covered book of 1930s fairytales open
on the quilt. Two planes over Brooklyn, a boy
my age the only survivor until the next day
when he died, too. I slid back into my fever

until *American Bandstand,* my five-year-old
sister staring silently at all those teenagers, me
too weak to dance with her, the air gone blue
outside. Mom lighting the broiler downstairs.

Vanishing Points

Only a few places really worked. The blue spruce next door
with its skirt of low branches brushing the ground. Its dark
hollow smelled of worms, wet earth, Christmas. Pine needles

got inside your socks and itched, but it was cool there even
mid-July. It hid you. Or high in the open air, a clearing on
the hilltop past your neighborhood's last house, half a sweaty

mile through the woods around a dead mansion. First a dim
tree-tunnel—nothing but wind and moving leaves—and then
the distant Hudson spread out like someone saying TA-DAH

past the iron call of anyone's mom's dinner bell. Two blocks
beyond where you were allowed to ride your bike was a street
full of kids you didn't know, flipping baseball cards in square

green yards. One girl called your name, but you pretended
not to hear her and pedaled away. Or the windowless cellar
under one house with its bend-down-low door, where boys

you'd played with for years suddenly tried to trick you to into
pulling down your pants. You wouldn't but still felt ashamed.
You never told your parents or went back. Also, the stories you

made up before sleep: three wishes. A million dollars and not
sharing it with anyone. Downstairs, the murmur of TV voices,
your mother's footsteps, your father's high, embarrassing laugh.

What I Want

I want to swim like I did when I was eight or nine
in the gentle chill of Cape Cod Bay, wallowing in water
that bleached the blood out of skinned knees and

mosquito bite bumps. (And stung at first, getting in,
but then didn't, my braids stuffed under a Kool-Aid-
smelling cap with rubber flowers of a violent hue

God never created. I understood this was for safety,
also knew my parents didn't watch closely after
the first ten minutes.) I want to dare myself out to

where I almost can't touch bottom anymore when
no one's noticing, my bottom—round as a fried clam—
popping up as I do the Dead Man's Float. Want to

coast on the wave I've been watching, ride it all the
way to sand and gravel, blasted by gritty mouthfuls,
even if water gets in my nose and I have to stand up

and snort it out, salty as canned soup. Want to shiver
when Mom finally drags me to the beach blanket: *Lord,
her lips are blue! She's going to freeze herself!* I'm

getting a *burn* (which I also wanted), hot and prickly
as that platinum squiggle of sun on the bay. Let's all
of us squint at it, make the entire world turn to magic.

On "Falling"

and now, still thousands of feet from her death she seems
To slow   she develops interest   she turns in her maneuverable body
                              —James Dickey, *Falling*

I was fourteen, holding steam-wrinkled pages
of *The New Yorker,* Breck-scented, tepid bathwater
foamy where I'd ducked my head under and come
back up to finish what I didn't want to but had to:

a woman at her job, an airplane's door blown
open, sucking her through to fall all the way to
the ground, fully conscious. I tried skipping lines
to end it faster. Couldn't. I was pulled into every

exacting word. It was like reading *Hiroshima,* but
that had been homework. This my parents had left
in our bathroom: a long poem that was also like
getting my first period, new and terrifying as my

breasts, those strange knife-points of desire that
woke up at all the wrong times and caused me
shame. I read the author's name again: a man,
animating a dead woman, wriggling her out of

her girdle on her way to dying, the heat of corn
fields pulling her down and down. I didn't know
how to be angry at him for such magnetic detail,
locking me into my own body. This stranger was

dreaming my death, too, in odd little word-gasps,
as if it were something to be savored, like the sex
I wasn't supposed to want, yet. He was saying
that if I tried to fly, a door might well blow out to

take me with it: mute, doomed. But he'd write
the story. I wouldn't even have a towel wrap up in.
And maybe the poem wouldn't actually be about
fucking, but its last two words would be OH GOD.

Making a 16mm Movie at the Cloisters

New York City, 1966

Of course my father took over the whole thing, made us
write a script with his corny idea, hovered too close as I
traced Romanesque arches with his old, wind-up camera.
Always his voice in my ear: *Slower, slower.* My best friend

Jane—who grew up to become a medievalist—she and I at
fourteen, in Independent Study. *Don't you want it to
look professional?* Light meters, the cost of black and white
film stock, our suburban high school's big experiment:

immerse us in The Humanities. *Slower, slower.* I didn't
want to listen to Dad and was afraid I'd fail if I did not.
All Saturday and passes to get out of class during the week,
the museum a long, lucid dream-chain: monasteries,

castles, altar pieces, tall stone walls, the camera alive,
whirring on the tripod—and above me a dark-eyed, angry
Byzantine Madonna inhabiting the high ceiling like God.
Slow down. It'll look faster onscreen. The stained glass

we couldn't afford to show in color, the Holy Virgin again
and again and again. It was the most beautiful place I'd
ever been, if I could just get rid of my father! Recordings
of Gregorian chant all echo and purity, stone floors

worn smooth by centuries of calm errands. Down the hill
New York City, still in its post-war polish and squalor. Such
rich stillness in that museum, silence and sound both so
gentled. *Slow down!* I wanted to live there and could not.

Fireworks

Be not wise in your own eyes before you have travelled through the way of foolishness, lest you may possess foolishness for wisdom
—Conrad Beissel

You're not supposed to love them but I do—
the home-made rockets arcing sideways
toward Lake Seneca and usually ending up
in Professor Somebody's rose bushes and

maybe he wasn't home and maybe we put it
out but I can't remember. Someone doing the
strange uphill walk of the young and drunk,
clutching a Genny Cream Ale tall boy, not

in much of a hurry, although he (always he)
had just lit something large with a match. The
special remote ignition system (created by
Someone Else who ended up teaching high

school chemistry in Florida) had failed. Again.
I'd ducked behind a mildew-smelling sea foam
green Ford convertible, behind an overgrown
barberry hedge, with thorns prickling my knees.

Someone yelling, *O, Shit! Incoming, incoming,
Incoming—lose the cap!* And laughing. The dead of winter
and still we burned punk and black powder. So
many steely stars above us in the vast peace

we had disrupted! Gloveless, hatless, our dun
green fur-hooded parkas flapping open, three
hundred miles from home, careless, smart
and very stupid. Allowed by Someone to survive.

Forsythia, 1973

I didn't want to leave my dorm room,
and knew I'd have to. It was late April.
In water glasses from the dining hall,
I was forcing forsythia, breathing in its

yellow, grassy no-scent, looking up from
Dubliners at blossoms rioting despite
Upstate's still-winter greys and browns,
where it could snow in May and I could

pretend I didn't have to go home to see
endless reruns of my parents' thousand
disappointments: the fury of my mother's
heartbroken jokes, my father's heavy step

past her, the screen door's metallic
slap as he carried his pitcher of martinis
outside. Slushy rain ticked my windows.
Down home, eye-stinging green pollen

already dusted the patio. On the wobbly
oak table I'd just bought at auction, a few
tiny blooms had dropped overnight. Tinier
leaves were already growing in. Soon,

I'd pull all my posters down, jam the table
into the back seat of my mother's Dodge.
Mom would be chipper; she loved taking
the five-hour drive up and back—away

from my father. Dreading the finals I knew
I'd do fine on, I wanted only the click of ice
needling glass on an endless, shadowless
afternoon. I didn't even want to turn the page.

What He Was Bad at He Did Anyway

My grandfather, my mother's father, poured milk
on his pie. His wife, daughter of the best pie baker
in Yonkers, NY, sang *O, there he goes again!* She

was Nana, he Gaga. Their fights weren't fights.
You'd put whipped cream on it, he said—no song,
just fact. And poured on more milk. He kept a tin

button box, did the sewing in their house, drove
their car, rewired bad sockets, built bird feeders
full of peanut butter, black seed, and lard. Let me

get lavishly sunburned playing in poison ivy, took
me rowing in leaky boats. What he was bad at
he did anyway, laughing. He had a withered arm

he barely used, was colorblind, didn't care. Salt
on the watermelon, a whole basket of swordfish
after deep sea fishing. An antler-handled knife to

carve pot roast and turkey. Scent of Noxzema and
hair pomade. Kodachrome slide shows of a month
in Florida, bags of the pure white beach brought

north in his Chevy Impala's trunk for my sandbox.
Every cat on our block found it. More laughter. In
my early twenties, he drove me through snow to

buy my first husband's Christmas present: a good
wooden recorder from Germany. Wouldn't let me
pay, then slid off the Cross Westchester Expressway

sideways. Stopped. Took a breath. *That flute okay?*
Yes. *You?* Fine. *Car seems alright.* More laughter. *Don't
tell your grandmother stories about this, you hear?*

Trying to Read *The Gulag Archipelago* on My First Hundred-Degree Day

Married to my first husband for one year, in our
apartment with only its bedroom air conditioned,

I waited until someone on TV announced it was
really one hundred degrees outside and walked

to the courtyard through our hall's airless murk
with the sole book on our shelves I hadn't read.

I sat under a crabapple tree on brown grass and
watched the afternoon sun spattering the ground—

bits of white heat that wobbled a little. There was
a breeze somewhere but I couldn't feel it. I wanted

to know what a hundred degrees felt like and this
was it: a desiccated leaf next to me that I crumbled

in my fingers and blew away. Sweat at the back of
my neck, under my hair and my breasts, even in

the shade. An icy mountain of a book I could not
manage to read and still haven't. Luminous green

bottles of beer inside, in the noisy refrigerator with
the chicken for dinner and a marriage that showed

no signs of failing, yet. Everything for the first time,
trying to make it all part of me, to breathe in and hold.

Junk Cedar

Sometimes, when enough time has passed,
you don't know who you are anymore. The sun is
pleasing in the red-budded tree behind the scraggly
cedar your sister always wants to take down, and

today you see the cedar for what it is: leggy, more
prickly needles than glory. Not a Californian guru
transplanted to New York, as you tried to imply
while she combed its tiny brown stickers from her

dog's long, white fur. You know it's a messy tree,
branches dropped next to your house in storms
carelessly as clothing around the unmade bed
the winter you first met your husband, the winter

it just kept snowing. You're pretty sure that cedar
was never even meant to be a tree, that it was
most likely a shrub planted beside a footpath at
least a century ago. Now even the footpath is gone.

When you cut down a tree, your sister tells you,
you get to see the long view beyond it. But what
were you meant to be? Sometimes, when enough
time has passed, you think you weren't meant to

be anything, that you just grew into who you are,
graceless as a junk cedar blocking the long view,
convulsed by early spring wind, hands high over
its head, laughing way too hard at its own joke.

Home Renovation Show

Stained wallpaper from the 1930s—faded green and coral,
lush with blowzy roses and garlands—gets a good laugh

before it's smashed into dust, fuzz tone guitars wailing.
Someone jumps feet-first right through it. The oak trim

someone else's mom teetered on an old stool to lemon oil
is *too much wood.* Paint it all white. Tear out the absurd

basement toilet her husband visited every morning with
his cigar and newspaper, undisturbed by its lack of walls.

Sledgehammer the black and white tile upstairs, blow out
a bedroom, install white marble and glass. Tell a lie: no one

ever lived here. Or cried herself to sleep. No one shattered
a pitcher of iced tea on the kitchen floor and was instantly

forgiven. No one ever, homework done at last, eased into
the bathtub with curly script on its HOT and COLD faucets.

No one's nana ever washed her back with a warm cloth
and fragrant, transparent glycerin soap. No one ever died.

Coming Back to Lead a Writing Workshop at the School Where I Once Worked

Praise the mutilated world and the gray feather a thrush lost
—Adam Zagajewski

Laminated directions sat on the teacher's desk next to her spare glasses,
a mug of cough drops, controls for the white board: *If the violence comes to*
your secured space, it's okay to try to escape. I tried to write with the kids

to poems I'd brought in: Bly, Akhmatova, Zagajewski. Tried to turn dust
motes into sequins in a slant of morning light, tried to find a small specific
worthy of praise. Colors, objects, articles of clothing: a girl with an oversized

green plaid shirt, a fuzzy-haired boy with the start of a beard. *Lock the doors,*
turn out the lights, take attendance, take instructions from law enforcement,
not announcements on the PA. We'd just started the drills the year I retired,

squatting in closets, cops in the loud hall shooting blanks to
    desensitize us
one conference day when all the kids were gone. If the violence
    comes, try to
praise something. A girl called on Bly's hard-of-hearing angels,
    called on

Jesus and Allah. Praise the warm morning, the radiators and the
    window
air conditioner running at the same time, the haze on the distant
    hills, empty
trees struck green and pink at their tips. Praise two black-haired
    nerdy girls

making jokes about Shakespeare, the kids I used to teach who are
    teachers
now themselves, the poetry slam in the library with the other local
    high school,
the tar-melting sun in the parking lot. Praise the violence that did
    not come.

At Brunch, My Mother Tells Me to Write About Mountains

I told her I had to write a poem today, and asked what
it should be about. *Mountains,* she said. I wondered
if that meant a landscape. *Any particular mountains?*

She said no. *Why mountains?* I sipped my white wine,
which made her pick up her iced coffee. *Because they're
nice to see, but I don't like climbing them.* To the best

of my knowledge, my mother has never, in her 94 years,
climbed a mountain. *Maybe in a car counts,* I thought.
Popocatépetl! said my husband. *That's a volcano, too!*

Leave it to a man to suggest a volcano, I thought. Mom
laughed at the word "Popocatépetl." He said it again.
She laughed harder. Which was fine. By then I was hiking

through a steep field in Arosa, Switzerland: blue sky,
wildflowers, cowbells, twenty years ago, winded, dizzy.
In my ears was *The Mysterious Mountain Symphony*

of Hovhaness, its awestruck French horns. Maybe I was
on my way to a mountaintop house with a tall fireplace
and many windows. Great distances opened before me,

then more mountains: brown and blue and white, calm
as Sphinxes, afternoon shadows passing over them like
a magician's hands. My husband and my mother were

still laughing. I was the one taking life too seriously,
scared witless on its narrow uphill road, lost as usual in
the sunny dazzle of nothing, that deep, deep mountain air.

My Mother

My sister says it helps if you think of my mother as
a baby, or a Zen master, totally in the moment, not

the woman who boiled my stuffed animals when I got
ringworm from digging in the yard at eight, playing

archeologist. Not the woman who splashed hot water
in her eye fishing out of that pot the toy dog I slept with.

Not the one who squinted at me, hissing wounded anger.
Not the mother of my poor effort at the times tables, not

the sigh and frown in Lord and Taylor's dressing room
at my unladylike sixth-grade belly. Maybe the one who

forgave me for reminding her of my dad and for getting
divorced. As if. As if. As if either of us could change

anything. Mother of my confirmation dress and veil,
mother of my first period, who handed me a pamphlet

produced by one of her company's clients advising
extra care in applying makeup on "those days." It said

nothing about blood. Mother of my never mentioning
that to her, even as a joke. Mother of my driving too fast

to her house when she fell, when her roof leaked, when
she forgot something new, when my father panicked.

You have a special relationship with your mother,
he'd say. *She'll listen to you.* Mother of the pills she

wouldn't take for me, either. Mother of the pills she
stuffed into her bra instead. My mother. My mother.

Jimmy Carter Released from the Hospital After Fracturing His Pelvis

October 24, 2019

Today is like Seattle, my sister says—sky of dun
clouds, sky like a forgotten world, sky like the family
we will or will not become after my mother dies.

My mother is Jimmy Carter's age and knits things
she alone sees in her long, eyes-open sleep, counts
pills, plays an absent piano, tells someone (maybe

my father, who died five years ago) *Get out of here!*
Bit by bit, it all falls away: the leaves—purply-red,
wet, slick, you have to take care walking—but also

my signature, no longer needed for identification.
I scribble a smiley face or peace sign on the screen
at the market. Divorced, remarried, I never know

my real name anyway. I am experimenting with not
needing my mother. Today, she wakes and smiles, she
who once scowled and swore she'd tell our pediatrician

I'd greed-gobbled an entire chocolate cupcake and
smeared it on his careful stitches near my lip: *He'd be
so disappointed!* Needing stitches was my fault, too,

but the dog who bit me is now dead as his master,
our neighborhood's lone bachelor, who'd warned me
not to get close or touch, who had the first color

TV on the block. Childless, he watched Walt Disney
every Sunday night anyway. You could stand next door
and see through his window. I still have a small scar,

but Mom and I have little left unfinished. Maybe I'll
give out Halloween candy on her porch, let her doze.
Jimmy Carter, bless him, plans to recuperate at home.

On the Glide Path

Sometimes I think my life has been a photograph
of a photograph, that I have been protected from

the unthinkable nearby explosion, from the smell
of house fires and shattered stone by what? Hate

or love? Or is it just fate shrugging: Thursday, not
Friday, here and not Syria? I think of my mother's

parents young, my mother a teenager, of her teasing
the local air raid warden in well-off, uphill Yonkers,

slipping through neatly mown backyards, laughing
as everyone else pulled down their blackout shades

because it could have happened here, it could have.
But it didn't. Not to her, not to me—although today

feels like the safety of the whole world is delicate as
water before the wind. My sister says *Mom is on the*

glide path now, and we've both started saying that:
seatbelts on, tray tables up, ready for landing. But

Mom's cheerful when she wakes most mornings:
eats breakfast, chats, then goes back to sleep. Her

oxygen concentrator beats out a guided meditation
if I time my breath to it: tick, beat. Tick, beat. She's

in no hurry. I couldn't have survived The Blitz. I'd
have been broken by the firestorms just a few nights

after Christmas. I don't need a blackout shade to make
my world darker. So why am I thinking of Churchill's

bunker, the Nazis bombing, sirens, and searchlights?
I get up to stretch and check: Mom is still breathing.

Driving North with My Husband

We do it without even meaning to, compass-
needled, heading away from The City and its
shimmer of too many voices, its comforting
galaxies of lighted apartment windows. North is

where we go when there's nothing to think about
but loss. There are fewer and fewer leaves and
then the trees are pencil-sketched against the
usual autumnal cloud-boulders, naked as fingers

without gloves. Of course it's cold. Wappinger's,
Mount Beacon, Fishkill. The cemetery Ken and
my mother visited to trace my family—what,
twenty years ago? That long? The abandoned

shopping mall, the giant, brick ruins of the
Hudson River State Hospital near Hyde Park,
the backhoes demolishing it stilled for Sunday.
The dark coming earlier than last week, that frank

loneliness. How deep it is up here! What a relief
not having to talk about it! The farm stand where
we stop to buy evergreens for our front porch.
The smoke of a wood stove. The smell of apples.

Dinner Time

It used to be something you wedged between
riding your bike endlessly up and down the street
and then going back outside into an afterward

already getting shorter and shorter before the
time change. The different bells different
families kept beside their back doors, the fathers

who could shrill a two-finger whistle half a mile,
the sun a red-gold ripple on the dining room
wall. The dining room! The everyday china—

not the good holiday stuff, something printed
with pink flowers. A glass of milk. Pot roast took
forever to chew. Spitting it out not an option.

The adults actually enjoying it. Talking, talking.
Jello for dessert: scarlet, unidentifiable: cherry?
The Redi-Whip can in your mother's hand, that

sound, that zip—and not as much as you'd have
taken if they'd let you but of course they didn't.
You hadn't been hungry. You weren't full now.

You didn't know what hunger felt like then.
The slam of someone else's screen door, the
chance to maybe grab an hour of coasting on

your bike, standing up on the pedals, singing
whatever dumb song everyone else sang. The
smile you give your mother's hired caregiver

now. You need to cook dinner for your husband;
everyone understands that. Makes it okay to
say thank you, to leave. Your real hunger: these

days you keep forgetting to eat. The dark, busy,
wet road, the long line of tail lights merging
on the TZ Bridge, the radios murmuring treason.

I Was Sad This Morning and Now I Am Not

The day still ahead of me, I mourned every
wild animal trapped for our amusement: all
the snakes and bright birds, boxed, sold, not
understanding. I mourned every person waiting

to not be lonely anymore and understanding the
hopelessness of that wait. Even the sun, where
it lit the woolly edges of grey clouds—even that
seemed sad. *He never apologizes. That's his*

secret, said someone in a news interview, and
I thought of other cruelties: the manufacture
of armaments, the will to use them, braggarts
laughing with guns in their hands. I visited

my mother then. She can't remember anything
but smiled when I told her I had to go home
and get some writing done. She wasn't sad,
so I wasn't either. She told me to watch out

for lunatics on the road and I told her *I'm
Gloria Blanck's daughter. The lunatics will
have to watch out for me.* That's when my life
slid back over me like a sweater, and I was fine.

After

After a long day in the house where I grew up,
watching my mother sleep in her recliner and
wake to ask if it's time for bed yet, after a long
day in a tall-ceilinged Victorian room that was

somehow both overheated and drafty, where
the TV was always, always on. After the whine
of that TV, its too-bright screen, the perky TV
cooks and newscasters and weather people,

after the weird echo of the same station from
the kitchen as my mother's aide chopped carrots.
After my mother awakened again and said,
This is just a quiet day, Christine, right? We

don't have to do anything, do we? After I said
No, of course not, and she said, *good,* she was
just going to take a nap. After the smell of soup
being heated. After I forgot the phone calls I

meant to make and forgot to look at my email
even though I had my phone and my laptop.
After I remembered blowing out the back door
fifty years ago, into the early winter night and

its soothing chill. After how angry I was then,
how hurt, after my young mother said, *Go on,
get out.* Long after all that. That's when I got up
to kiss my mother on her cheek and she smiled.

It was early winter again and the outside air
was a kiss back. Behind me, yellow light from
the kitchen slanted out onto the porch. After I
got in my car, my old neighborhood was pretty,

well-dressed for the dark. That's when I saw it:
high above empty trees and rush hour traffic,
a shooting star's long, silent arc streaking
into ashes and nothing, dissolving into the sky.

My Sister's Birthday Is the Day After 9/11

And on it, twenty years after all that dying, I read
about the last person found alive in the rubble of
Ground Zero, a woman who still believes an angel
took her hand and pulled: a rebirth. I wish I could

have given Susan that for a present twenty years
ago, when we finally got email to each other; she
was stuck in Italy, I awake all night in New York,
smelling what we all did when the wind shifted.

I wish I could have said, "It wasn't an angel truly
but here is someone who lived, for your birthday."
When our mother died for four months, my sister
sat at her side for my birthday: two late September

nights on the Jersey Shore, my phone of course
ringing the first morning: Mom worse, not wanting
breakfast, not getting up. *No, stay down there with
Ken. Who's to say it'll be today? She could die with*

you stuck in traffic! Or not. Not on your birthday, though, please. At least have your birthday. The ocean went about its steady business at my feet as I gazed out into all that gray: shush, shush, shush.

And so I stayed. Back in New York, my sister's friend Joshua arrived to perform all the Bach Cello Suites so my mother could take peaceful leave of herself. He kissed her hand when he was done. But

Mom opened her eyes and walked into the kitchen to eat dinner. How many angels are there in this story? And how many birthdays? How many bright, indifferent clouds drift in a wind we cannot see?

My Late Mother Drinking Apple Martinis with J.S. Bach

She'd have never admitted this is what she'd want
Heaven to be, but maybe Heaven's what you can't
admit wanting and are simply granted. Maybe her

Heaven looks like her kitchen before we tried to fix
it up so much. The drinks she's poured into two tiny
crystal cocktail glasses burn emerald in the window's

autumn light. *My old friend Bea showed me how
to make these,* she tells Johann. He lifts one in silent
toast to her, then sips. *They are so . . . smooth,* he says.

I don't know what language they are speaking, but
he does have a German accent. She's just played *The
Magnetic Rag* by Scott Joplin on her old baby grand—

made two mistakes—but he just laughed and said
Go on, go on. She opened her mouth to apologize
but realized there was no need to. He says he's met

Scott Joplin—a fine gentleman—would she like an
introduction? She rests her wedding ring hand on
the old Formica counter with its fake gold veins, and

everything sparkles in the sun. *These taste just like
fruit juice,* Johann says. *Might I have another?* Mom
chuckles. *Just a little healthy fruit juice. I'd love to

meet Scott Joplin.* Ice cubes clatter in the shaker.
My father's in the living room, talking politics with
somebody important and not yelling. My sister and I

are in the lovely background. I've even managed to
stay married. My mother has forgotten needing our
help—or anyone else's. She has forgotten forgetting.

On the Seven Canonical Hours

*O, Lord open thou my lips and my mouth
shall show forth thy praise*
—Psalm 51

Since the fifth century, someone has been praying this, always.
It's like the wind this morning that comes from everywhere

and hammers our shutters against our house, like drafts that
get in around our windows, like new sunlight that is sharper

each day with the coming of winter. Everything that shaded us
over the summer is being scraped away, flying and tumbling,

wings without birds. And with them, lauds, terce, vespers,
night watch, the slow caress of the sun over our foolishness.

Open thou my lips and I will praise thee. Praise my fear, my
shaky witness, the thrill of seeing more than I wanted to, even

the ugly parade of white trucks on the bridge over the Hudson.
which tried for but did not earn my fear. Praise the faithful dead,

the constant, daily sweep of the hours, the astonishing energy
of every heart in the world. Praise dawn every day. What planets,

what pinprick distant star, what shivery moonlight? What water,
frozen or free, what tides! Open thou my lips and I shall praise
    thee.

Some Facts You Should Know About the Love of Music

Johann Sebastian Bach had a street brawl with a student
whose bassoon he'd insulted and who was therefore trying

to brain him with a stick. Tchaikovsky and Saint Saëns liked
impersonating ballerinas together. Bach was carrying a knife.

Tchaikovsky was almost certainly gay, Saint Saens, too.
The student's clothing was shredded before his friends

pulled Bach off him. Tchaikovsky's wife could not have
comprehended the words describing homosexuality. A 20th-

century composer of organ music named Richard Purvis
wrote an arrangement of "Greensleeves" in a fox hole, under

live fire, during World War II. Saint Saëns eventually left
his wife. Tchaikovsky did, too. Richard Purvis led the first

military band through liberated Paris after his rescue from
a German POW camp. His "Greensleeves" sounds like the

whole world's broken heart, trying to bear up. A grave robber
stole Hayden's skull. So it was replaced with someone else's

but later found. Now there are two. The judge let Bach's
student go and instructed Bach to be more likable. Music

is the last thing to leave anyone with dementia. Bach and
Handel were blinded by the same inept surgeon. My own

mother, before her diagnosis of terminal kidney disease, sat
in her doctor's office, singing "Flat Foot Floozy," out loud.

Preacher's Traveling Organ

It probably survived by being broken, never
wired-up for someone's psychedelic band
in the 60s, not interesting to children who'd
have abused it casually as they do aged dogs

they are told not to bother. Shaped like a tiny
chapel itself: black wood, tarnished gilt, legs
meant to fold under so it could be carried.
Weak and tired as any of us are when love

surprises us and we find ourselves needed
once again. My husband has repaired it and
playing it is like riding your first bicycle uphill
on a warm day full of white-flowering trees,

or maybe like your grandmother's voice, not
when she was scolding you but when she
sang the alleluias from "The Strife Is O'er,"
and freed your hair from the braids you hated

so she could brush it for you. See? It's just the
two of you in your bedroom, after supper, and
the shades are pulled down against the length
of the light. She stands behind you, lost in song.

Singing Solo

I used to love it, at least in theory
or rehearsal, my own voice stone-wall
bounced, loud as waves on the beach
on a day you're glad to be there. *This*

is a good room, my husband would say;
It'll fix anything you do wrong. He'd
be right. He'd play the organ and I'd
sing in Latin, amazing myself with that

ballgown of a language: something I
never thought I'd wear, a fancy party
I crashed, perhaps. *Soli Deo gloria,*
and flipping your "r's" is not affected

even if your sister rolls her eyes. He
taught me that so I sang, his wife
and student. Now I like it best when
it's all over, music in a messy pile

he'll file later, the two of us equally
into a plate of fried calamari at City
Island, eating with our hands, praise
be to God and perhaps a second beer.

Magdalene

You have to go back before the paintings. Before
the woman in the long red dress, weeping, both
breasts exposed. Before the early Church fathers

made a whore of her. She had her own money and
financed things, was smart and understood things,
or was at least brave enough to go to the Tomb in

the blue twilight before dawn, with the Sabbath
over at last—if there really were a Tomb, a Stone
or an Angel. If Pilate would have even permitted

such a burial. If the men—always men—writing
the accounts had any desire to tell the truth. In
a broken fresco painted two hundred years later,

Mary's arm is bent, her eyes wide open, the great
Stone still heavily in place. Something is clearly
about to happen. Consider the ghosts of buildings

revealed on other buildings in renovations: traces
of lost walls and roofs, places people lived: now you
can see them again, but you also have to imagine.

You can't help but imagine. Her sandals, the vial
of perfume she carries with her, the empty street,
an ox stomping his forefoot in the cool morning air.

My Cat Talks in Her Sleep

Little chirps, half-mews, paws twitching,
sometimes her tail, the whorl of her black and
grey stripes shuddering like water in the breeze

just before a storm. She adjusts her head—still
sleeping—then descends further and is quiet as
the rest of the house in which we are alone, she

and I. I sit in my office, my whole life a series
of stories like tidied rooms, grateful for such
comfort and silence. Soon, it will begin to snow

again and my husband will return from the job
he still loves. What have I forgotten to love, today?
The low, grey sky, the distant rumble of a train.

The Noisy Person I Am

I can't be the noisy person I am if you don't stop talking
—Robert Bly

My husband says married people need to listen
to each other's stories, even the ones we have heard
five times before, the ones you can tell are coming
by your own sorrow and the time of the evening:

the acre of tobacco planted, the uncle who fell
off the distillery roof, the suicide by kerosine
and fire, the suicide in the cold river. The entrance
exam aced, the first night living in New York City.

My husband says I might as well ride to Trenton
past everything that's ruined in New Jersey as
keep getting on the train West and back East
to watch some farmer stoking his burn pile,

the smoke of which I can't smell at two minutes
after three this clay-clouded afternoon on
The Empire Builder—and the farmer doesn't
even look up to see the train. My husband's father

was a farmer. Why don't I daydream about Italy?
Even the train is telling me an old story. Surely
I have heard this one before. But it's loose-woven
and there's room for me in it. I can tell my own

at the same time and nobody gets offended.
Here it is: these great flat plains are the color
of a lion's haunches and go on for keeps. I miss
my husband, but I am not quite ready to go home.

Snapshots with Strangers

I think of people whose pictures I have taken but
never spoken to—the shoulder in a red t-shirt just
past my husband's plate of fried oysters, or someone
on the Cabot Trail fifteen feet in front of us, head so

engulfed by a white blaze of sun that I can't tell you
anything more: a hiker. Easter four years ago—a
dark-haired couple in the dark pub after Good Friday
night services. They were laughing together. I don't

know if they'd met that night or had been married
for a decade. We were laughing, too, despite the date;
the cable to the church bell had frayed and broken
while we were tolling thirty-three, taking from Jesus

three or four years of earthly life. My husband was
ringing and he'd come out of the tower giggling, with
rope looped around himself like a cape—or a noose.
Likely, we're all in the background of someone else's

snapshot, unknowing. We are laughing even though
at the next table, somebody's father has just died, or
one day soon, someone else will run a fever and then
too many of us will. We'll still take pictures, though—

See? I got here—masks dropped to show our smiles,
slate-colored mountains behind us, a lake full of boats
newly launched for the summer, that squinty glitter.
I finally made it here—and all of you along with me.

What We Really Lost

Everything. At first, it didn't seem real, as if the clouds in the sky
had suddenly become puppets. There weren't even bombers,
but then a dozen nuns and priests died at a gray stone convent
across the gray Hudson. And after that, a woman who had taught

with my husband at the elementary school in our town, her
whole family, every one of them, all. By then there were barely
airplanes. The traffic on our street had stopped. Birds called out
in the springtime heat and other birds answered them. Nightly,

the TV showed us pictures of the Empire State Building, tip
lit bloody red, like an ambulance, in tribute to the doctors
and nurses who had died. And also for those still at work, dull-
eyed, the skin on their faces mottled by their masks. Many

borders closed. No one was in charge. It was always 11 AM
or 3 PM and it didn't matter. The names of the dead became
more and more familiar. Then we had to get tested ourselves
and somehow escaped. *Everything* was a heart that burst then,

but even this season's funerals are mercy: a mother, a father.
For now we have permission to sing in public. But the sun's
cheery sizzle, its long kite-string of joy—how uncertain that
all feels today! Patience. We are still learning what we can trust.

And then, after you got the vaccine

you didn't want to limp, even though your creaky
knee makes that happen sometimes and the hall
to the door outside felt long. Your knee didn't
hurt before you spent a year inside—exercising, yes,

but with bands and balls and a prescription. You'd
actually feared the men hiking past you at the lake,
their unmasked nostrils suddenly obscene. The hall
felt long and it was still daylight but barely when you

pushed the door at the end of it open, your fingers
reeking of New York State Clean from the gallon jug
with its plunger applicator, and cold with its alcohol—
a scent like a cheap head shop. Then the many white

Art Deco steps of the Westchester County Center.
The harmless man in a wheelchair on the sidewalk:
masked, your age. The chipped paint on the iron
railing. You were a little girl in this place once. At

last, turning the corner as if it were all nothing, your
husband, eyes brightening as he sees you. His long
stride you'll have to hurry to match—but his eyes. This
thing won't kill you now. Rush hour. The ride home.

On the National Day of Mourning for the Covid Dead

Somehow, I'm thinking cotton candy, Marie Antoinette's
bouffant, but all girly-girl pink on a paper cone. And huge!

Even bigger than my head! How it dissolved into nothing
as I tried to eat it! I'm thinking wet grass under our plaid

blanket in the mosquito-bite twilight of a Cape Cod brass
band concert. I was six, standing on my father's sneakers.

He was teaching me how to jitterbug. Mom said he always
stepped on her toes when they danced, but he said to step

on his. I didn't understand. My teeth stuck together
by melted sugar, my face sticky. Other kids with balloons,

balloons let go into stars and darkness. I held his hands
and tried to keep my balance. Then Mom laughed but I

could tell she was sad about something. Suppose everything
I've written until now had simply dissolved into nothing?

One hundred thousand people. I'm dancing on all of their
shoes, trying to keep my balance. I still can't understand:

all that sugary twilight gone, all that lost music. Mothers,
fathers. Other kids. Balloons let go into stars and darkness.

Awakening Around Three, Lovestruck

Why is it so easy to love someone who is asleep,
so important to listen to his breath as he sleeps?
The cat who also loves my husband stretches and

turns his sullen bronze eyes on me. My waking's
an intrusion on the watch he has kept for hours.
Outside, the sky has opened its wooly coat and

stars have tumbled from all its drunken pockets!
How dare I only notice the cold rain has stopped?
Tomorrow morning, when our wet roof steams in

spring's sudden heat, Ken will walk downstairs
saying (as always), *dreams, dreams, dreams.*
Later, we'll probably annoy each other. By then,

the cat will be asleep in a yellow wash of sun and
somehow, we'll all travel through what we must.
Mercy, Lord. No part of me wants to be practical.

Blessed Are Those Who Mourn

Blessed are those who mourn, for they will be comforted
—Matthew 5:4

There is no loss more bitter than a bell's
final strike, that last overtone echoing harshly—
a minor third, my husband tells me, minor even

when you are not tolling a funeral, even when it's
a wedding instead. Or a baptism, or playing music
on a carillon: a minor third at the end but then only

the wet street, the sibilance of traffic, people on their
way somewhere else. The end of things, when there's
no more to announce or embellish. Even the Queen

sits by herself in a choir stall without her crown,
wearing a black suit and hat, all that heavily carved,
oaken, nine-hundred-year-old space around her,

like the sigh at the end of a story. You have to listen
to that, stop talking and listen. The time will come
when the bells stop, and you will hold your hands

before you in a wind untouched by any sunrise. You
will need to have faith that it will warm, even if that
seems impossible. And you will have to do it alone.

Blessed Are the Merciful

Blessed are the merciful, for they will be shown mercy
—Matthew 5:7

Before the sun rose, the morning after John Lennon
was murdered just forty minutes down the Hudson
from where I was waking up in my first post-divorce
apartment, I probably didn't stop and notice how

at five a.m. in December, darkness turns windows into
dead letters, so no view of the world gets delivered,
only blackness, and I'd have been especially blind
after the glare of the bathroom tiles, the steam of the

shower. I know I put on my work boots and hiked
a mile and a half to open the kitchen at the school, just
behind two old Haitian women strolling arm in arm,
but talking fast. I hadn't turned on news, not wanting

to wake my roommates, and I'd gone to bed early
because of my job. By then the sky was a little pink.
We were far enough into town for streetlights. When
one of the old women said *Il est mort,* I began to run,

ran past them to a deli just unlocking for the day,
and read tabloid headlines and stood in the yellow
light that pooled out onto the sidewalk, forgetting
to order coffee. The air was business-like and cold.

I kept walking, wondering how early I could call a
man I thought I was in love with, someone who didn't
love me back. He'd be no comfort, and I would forgive
him that. I'd start work with all the stardust drained out

of me, turn on ovens, lights, a quiet radio. I'd be where
I belonged, slicing bread, breaking eggs. Still, in my
sorrow, I'd see no mercy—even in the feathery grey
ripples of the river brushing the cheek of the new day.

How Hate Spreads

Like the seasons change—a little
and then a lot. The way the trees
start out naked but suddenly the
7 a.m. light ripples with shadows

of baby-green leaves. Just like that.
Like something so pretty it slides
right past you. Eat it in the sun with
your brother at a hamburger stand

on the road you've driven happily
forever. The breeze through your
thrown-wide windows may be
sweet as the first beach day on a

long vacation, but hate beats like
a second heart in everyone's chest.
The day after one election, you
felt a hundred funerals at the desk

where you still work today. That
was before things sprouted. Now
you're angry when you're not angry.
Now, the news is on at four and six

and nine. You think of the woman
you saw begging between lanes of
jammed-up cars on the FDR Drive.
Your phone's traffic app labeled her

a hazard. You looked away. You want
to rip out hate like bindweed, but here
it comes again in the tight-wrapped
purple buds of lilacs, all ready to bloom.

Sparrows, Starlings

Are not five sparrows sold for two pennies?
And not one of them is forgotten before God.
                              —Luke 12:6

Consider the tiny hard-eyed birds in the skylight of the shopping
    mall,
shoe-leather brown, fat on french fries, the cast-off bits of hot
    dogs, sodden
ends of ice cream cones, and mean as a sore knee—or the ones
    dining

outdoors with you, bullying their way into croissants and spilled
    lattes. One
lights on the table two feet from your shopping bag and turns its
    head right
and then left, puffing its feathers: *Give me.* A house sparrow, its
    species now

in decline in its native England. Supposedly loosed upon Central
    Park in
the nineteenth century by Eugene Schieffelin, who may or may not
    have been
trying to seed America with every bird mentioned by Shakespeare.
    Bees

hum in the garbage can beside the only other unoccupied seat. Best
    to
carry your coffee to the car and drive home, where starlings the
    color of
oil puddles and stippled at the neck by metallic rainbows shovel
    seed from

your feeders onto the ground. Descendants of another flock
    brought here by
the same man, but handsome, sleek as new-sharpened pencils.
    Nest-robbers,
though. And neither breed protected by U.S. law against human
    cruelty, not

like other wild birds. Common. Aggressive. Destructive. Weed-
    creatures.
And yet if you had never before seen wings work you'd forgive
    them for
being here with the rest of us, the result of our good intentions and
    folly.

As if they need forgiveness. Great numbers of starlings fly
    sometimes in the
shapes of wings or even whole birds: undulating murmurations;
    dark,
shimmering clouds—like songs you can see. The way prayers look
    to God.

On the Election

*How long, dear Savior, oh how long
shall this glad hour delay?*
   —Jeremiah Ingalls, *Northfield*

I am afraid and I am resolved. The sky is cloudy again
and the leaves have sponged up the light left behind.
It's getting dark but there is no darkness in the trees.

My sister told me she was hired once as an editor
because the man interviewing her believed her capable
of talking someone out of a Turkish jail. I couldn't do that.

I'd just see it coming: the folly, the arrest, the clamor
of a dusty street I can barely imagine. Some people say
I worry too much. Before the last Presidential election,

I saw two men, feet planted firm in front of a church
at the top of a hill where two busy roads intersected.
The men held banners longer than they were tall and

waved them out over traffic like a curse that was sure
of itself. *Fly swift around ye wheels of time!* We will
decide what we will decide and then it will be winter.

It's dusk now, so I watch by the light of what's left:
one last summer-red spray of roses lost in the garden's
collapse: marigolds, nasturtiums, a sparrow pecking seed.

Another Poem About the Fourth of July

I don't even know what I can say about it anymore, now
that I'll never again drop a pack of lighted ladyfingers

down a Manhattan apartment building's airshaft and
crazy-run to the elevator behind my screaming-laughing

college roommate. Lately, even polite fried chicken
and homemade peach pie seem like overkill. Truth is,

I'm usually away from home, the glittering fingers of
a local fireworks display surprising me after hamburgers

on a motel balcony, the antique fire trucks and Girl Scouts
having long since paraded, everything over by the time

I think to look. Abroad, it's even stranger: two or three
distant skyrockets in Berlin, some fellow Yank shooting up

the sky over the Gulf of St. Lawrence near the national park
on Prince Edward Island. I remember the red streaks of

taillights on ring roads around Washington DC, the tooth-
pale Lincoln Memorial lights, on all night. Crowds scattering,

people walking back to their cars by themselves: a loneliness
that doesn't even know how lonely it is. There's patriotism

in that, but it's not easy to celebrate because you have to love something you can't even name: a forgotten promise, a dense

July night, old houses lining American rivers. The gilded domes of darkened civic buildings, the silence that divides our dreams.

I Want to Love the World

I want to love the world but I'm tired of it
walking by me on the street and not
even waving. And making so much noise

late at night. It's a parked car with closed-
tight windows and the radio thumping.
It's been outside my house for weeks. How

can you think of anything else with all
that artillery? I want to love the way early
afternoon looks on the stone floor of my

office, how pollen's dust on my windows
casts a golden shadow. But that only
reminds me it's getting later and now I

can't tell you what I was trying to say. The
world has interrupted me. And why should
it care about that? I want to love the world

but I'm tired. In Kyiv, the coroner burns
church incense. To each face he uncovers,
he says, *How? How did this happen to you?*

I Can't Lie to You

Why should I trick you with daisies
and pastels? Peace is not a blue flag
applauding a blue sky, not the two or
three hundred encircled arrows I drew

without even thinking about it on my
notebook in 1969. Truth is, we're all
angry. We all woke up afraid and were
left alone to cry it out. Someone once

raised a loud, deep voice to us, so now
we recruit armies. We're all looking
for a false dawn: that yellow line of
light at the bottom of our shut-tight

bedroom doors as our parents drink
downstairs. We hear the rising tide
of their laughter, smell the enticing
bonfires of their cigarettes. But they

don't hear us call to them. And we
pretend we don't remember. I can't
lie to you. Peace sits by herself on the
breathing ocean's other side, watching

over the darkness of a ruined city. She
texts neighbors who fled the war, phone
cupped like a candle in her fingers. Just
now, the full moon dissolves the clouds.

Close Call

I'm still not sure I really saw the car—shiny red
on a day that was a long green nap—go airborne.

I saw the utility pole it had hit tremble—testing
itself against electric wires that couldn't catch it—

and fall. But the car was surely on its roof and
beyond it the reservoir was lovely as that word's

sound, and full of springtime rain. And past that,
long suburban lawns, eighty different shades of

green, green that owned itself so proudly you'd
need a Geiger counter to say how green: crazy, a

neon green, Kelly green, green like tomato vines
about to blossom and bear fruit. So I called 911.

My husband got us parked and ran across the
street to the kid in the upside-down red car, who

we both thought must be dead. Who seemed that
profoundly still but moved his hands to put them

both over his face. It was raining again by then,
tiny drops you couldn't see, and there were wires

down on the wet pavement. The cop who helped
the kid stand up and walk to the ambulance that

arrived told us he heard those wires singing. We'd
known they must be live. I'm old, my husband too.

The measure of our lives stretches out like a silly
accordion. We understand any number of dangers,

often read the papers to find out about them. We
step carefully in these day-long dusks, this sugary,

constant May rain. But I think our country is still
a garden. Look, irises snap their purple fingers on

creek banks; somehow, kids flip their cars and live.
And somehow the wires are still singing with news.

I'll Tell You a Secret

I want to tell people that I am sure of my faith
so they will be sure of theirs, even if they
believe in something stupid. Maybe it's like

this noontime thunder: all the fussy blossoms
on the trees but so much rain that the air
actually looks bright because of it. See there?

The sky off to the south's iron-colored, full
of straight-out cursing. Oh, yeah. You think
that scares me? Actually, it does a little but

radar always looks worse than ground truth.
Maybe I want to see base reflectivity images
of God passing overhead. And maybe I don't.

Somebody said that metaphorical resurrection
wasn't enough for him, as if literal really is
more important. I'll tell you a secret: there's no

such thing as the literal, only the sudden rush
of this creek. Only the smooth, tight fists of the
stones in it, silently remembering everything.

Just Before Thanksgiving

Sometimes, it's like walking up many flights of stairs
slowly. Always dawn or sunset—hard to tell. Days
flutter like match flames but that's alright. You strike
another and another. You read an article about how

macaroni and cheese came from ancient Rome and
think of the glass baking dish you use and of pies and
what you still need to gather. Outside, wind punches
at the cedars. Today's air is brilliant and smells of

rosemary and wet earth. It got colder overnight. It
always gets colder overnight. You blame yourself for
not missing your parents more at holidays. You
imagine there are members of your family still alive

who absolutely do not miss you. What is it we say? *It's
just easier.* Nervous laughter. Silent nods. A family is
a thing that knows exactly how crazy everyone in it is.
Three people you know have died this week. You need

a can of pumpkin, a bunch of parsley if it didn't freeze.
A bottle of corn syrup, clear as gin. You need patience.
Need to bring the turkey stock in from chilling on the
deck. Need to believe there's a reason for all this light.

All of Us New to Caution

Pie-stunned, muffled under a meal we
almost couldn't finish, me finishing
a sepia-colored glass of Angel's Envy,

our friends three sets of headlights on
Route 9W—two north, one south. The
Hudson black as tarnished silver and

breathing like a cat asleep: I can say
that without even seeing it. Midnight
at twenty-five after eight. Ken and I

agreeing about the couple ready to
divorce but quiet and gentle today: all
for the best, but whatever will *he* do?

We six having gathered and dispersed,
white hair luminous in candlelight,
badass still, bad hips beside the point,

using words like *blotter acid* and *gig*
and *cop*. All of us new to caution but
not gratitude. When someone up on

Maple, just past the woods, began to
shoot skyrockets: stupid red and blue,
fiery dandelion seeds: *I'm so thankful*

I'm exploding! Not us, not anymore.
Shocked, empty tree branches lit too
bright. And then, quiet. No harm done.

The Feast of Busby Berkeley

Big holidays are often because of things
that weren't the disaster you'd imagine—
often events you wouldn't even notice

if you weren't paying attention: lots of
oil, a state execution foiled, death taking
its unfixable thievery elsewhere. The old

friend released from the hospital, the
Aurora showing its dragon-green dance
to a solitary teacher driving the reservoir

causeway on her way to school just before
dawn, radio in her car untouched by any
solar storm. And this black and white

movie: ninety years old, three hundred
showgirls camped overnight in an arena-
sized rehearsal hall, learning a new routine,

each of them equipped with a negligee,
swimsuit, and waterproof makeup: every bit
as crazy a story as you getting to watch it

now and stop mourning the news. You did,
too, after clicking a single button thrice.
Later you stepped out on the porch into air

deep with frost and midnight, taken by a
hilarious delirium. Everything hushed, the
creek shuffling water. So. Why not believe?

Mostly, I'm Thinking of Ghosts

I'm thinking again about the scrolled and stenciled
glass-shaded hurricane lamps in the basement of
my parents' first house, the sharp, interesting smell

of kerosine, the burned-black tip of their wicks, the
dull, yellow glow they cast upstairs, lit. They seemed
none too useful until you blew them out and saw how

dark the house was without electricity and a hurricane
stomping around outside. I'm thinking of how a big tree,
blown-over, could terrify, still-green branches splayed

on our lawn, roots pale as bleached bones escaping
a ragged hole in the grass. Or worse, a wounded animal,
angry and dangerous. I couldn't bear to look but still

wanted to feel wind on my skin. My father said *Get in;
it's seventy miles an hour!* But I was afraid of the tree,
not the wind. And I liked the way the stairwell looked as

my mother carried a hurricane lamp to bed, how the
walls swallowed its dusty light as she climbed. But mostly,
I'm thinking of ghosts. Thinking of my parents' ghosts,

the ghost of their love's cruel, unpredictable storm,
invisible but potent decades after it blew itself to
shreds in the open ocean beyond Cape Cod. Thinking

of my parents' last house, the one that almost never
lost its electricity, the house where they both died
in their nineties. Of how my goddaughter stayed there

afterwards, when she was first back in New York. She
slept in my father's old room on a dragged-in mattress
just before we sold the place. The weather was calm

but her tom cat stared at the door to the upstairs hall
all night and well into the mornings: someone was
walking there. *Look! Look at that! What is it he sees?*

All Our Houses Are the Same House

All our stories are the same story: it
gets dark and we light fires and lamps.
Seeds sleep under the snow. No one

really dies. Our grandparents come
out to meet us at the end of a long
sidewalk in the shade of tall bushes.

They fall to their knees, glad-crying
but then we awake. Except one day,
we don't awake. In the wind, the wind—

that's where everyone is, riding the
updraft, circling like the year's last
leaves. The door blows open and

no one knows why. But that's why.
Nobody's hung Christmas lights yet
but up and down the street, each

window goes yellow in the dusk. The
creek is slow and quiet. Seeds sleep
under the snow. No one really dies.

In these days, we're clothed only
with love. Someone is leaving and
someone is coming to the door. All

our houses are the same house. What
an honor to wait in it, listening. What
an honor to turn on the stove and cook.

Nana and the Squirrels

She really thought they were dead. That
was the story, but now she is—with both
my parents likewise departed—I'm left

to explain: Nana was my mother's mother.
Who loved wild birds and squirrels, which she
called *the animals*. Who kept few pets other

than a long line of caged finches named
Tiny Tim—all of them—not Tim the First or
Tim the Second, just Tiny Tim. One Tim at

a time. Late one winter, after the last Tim,
she grew tired of fruitcake. No one else
could stand to eat more of it, either. Still,

she preserved hers: tight-sealed in round,
fancy tins, brandied and re-brandied at least
weekly. I'm heady remembering wrenching

a lid open to inhale deeply: so many red
and green candied cherries, all sexed up,
too hot with alcohol to even taste. Was it

February? I see a cold, bright day, precise
shadows of empty trees and clotheslines
on her backyard's dormant grass, as Nana

chose to be done with Christmas, chose to
offer a Mardi Gras of fruitcake to her
bird feeder and the hard earth below it,

her fingers sticky-sweet, booze fumes rising.
The sparrows flew off, but the squirrel
community arrived in force, swinging on a

little wooden platform my grandfather had
built for breadcrumbs and seed. They hung
from every branch, frantic for nuts and

citron and raisins, grabbing fruitcake, tails
rolled against their backs, stuffing their cheeks
faster than I can type these words. Until they

lost grip and tumbled over and down, easy two
dozen or more—I wasn't there, only heard tell—
every squirrel on Roberts Avenue overcome by

hootch and love, stone-still, scattered like rags
in my grandmother's yard on a short, blue, winter
afternoon. And Nana crying, wailing *O, Eddie*

Eddie! to her husband, who took his chance and
laughed. His rough faith had told him they'd
sober up and regret nothing, lacking the word for

hangover. And he was right. O, Life, which we, too,
gobble! May we end up so grateful for your
intoxicating feast, so fearless of the nap to come.

Why I Don't Take Xanax

Because the sky outside right now is both
grey and violet and enough leaves are gone
so I can finally see it from my desk. Because

pills only teach you how to swallow. Because
it's late but not yet evening. Because my cat has
jumped off my desk and I can type without her

tail on the keyboard. Because there are too many
rattling bottles in the world and I do not want
another one, or anyone's permission to own it.

Because it's gotten dark but the sky is still violet.
Because my worries are two screech owls, talking
back and forth, somewhere up the valley. Because

screech owls are quite small and almost invisible
by day, with dappled grey feathers like tree bark.
Because 2 AM is relative and it's not 2 AM yet.

Because 2 AM passes like a stranger whistling
on his way home. Because I never wanted my
heart to walk a straight line in this magic world.

About the Author

Christine Potter is the poetry editor of *Eclectica Magazine*. She has also been a chef, a ringer of tower bells at churches, a chorister, and a high school English teacher.

Her poetry has appeared in *Eclectica, Rattle, Third Wednesday, Kestrel, Tar River Poetry, The McNeese Review, ONE ART, Does It Have Pockets, Autumn Sky Poetry Daily,* and many other publications. Her time-traveling young adult novels, The Bean Books, are published by Evernight Teen. Her last full-length collection of poetry, *Unforgetting,* is also on Kelsay Books.

Christine lives with her husband Ken, a few ghosts, and their indulged kitty Bella in a very old Hudson River Valley house.

www.ingramcontent.com/pod-product-compliance
Lightning Source LLC
Chambersburg PA
CBHW031420160426
43196CB00008B/1005